PIANO · VOCAL · GUITAR

TWILA PARIS

GREATEST HITS

ISBN 0-634-03717-X

HAL·LEONARD®
CORPORATION
7777 W. BLUEMOUND RD. P.O. BOX 13819 MILWAUKEE, WI 53213

Visit Hal Leonard Online at
www.halleonard.com

CONTENTS

GOD IS IN CONTROL

Words and Music by
TWILA PARIS

Steady, with drive

This is __ no time for
His - to - ry march - es

fear. This is __ a time for __ faith and de - ter - min - a - tion.
on. There is __ a bot - tom __ line drawn a - cross the __ a - ges.

Don't lose the vi-sion here, car-ried a - way by the mo-
Cul-ture can make its plan, oh, but the line nev-er chang-

-tion. Hold on to all that you hide in your heart. There is one
-es. No mat-ter how the de-cep-tion may fly, there is one

thing that has al-ways been true. It holds the world to-geth-er.
thing that has al-ways been true. It will be true for-ev-er.

God is in con-trol. We believe that His chil-dren will not be for-sak- en. God is in con- trol.

We will choose to re-mem- ber and nev-er be shak- en.

There is no pow-er a - bove or be-side Him. We

know, oh, God is in con- trol. Oh,

Lyrics:

God is in __ con-trol. __

He has nev-er let __ you __ down. __ Why start to wor-ry now? __ Why start to wor-ry now? __

__ He is still the __ Lord of all __ we see and

He is still _ the lov - ing Fa - ther, watch-ing o - ver you _ and me. _____

Watch-ing o - ver _ you. _ Watch-ing o - ver _ me. _

Watch-ing o - ver _ ev - 'ry - thing. _____ Watch-ing o - ver _ you. _

Watch-ing o - ver _ me. _ Ev - 'ry lit - tle spar - row, ev - 'ry lit - tle

C
Fsus/C
E♭/C
king,
oh,
F/C
C
Fsus/C
ev - 'ry lit - tle
king.
E♭/C
F/C
Oh.
G
D
C
God is in con - trol.
We be - lieve that His chil - dren will

D G D
not be - for - sak - en. God is in con - trol. We will
C D G/B
choose to re - mem - ber and nev - er be shak - en. There is no pow - er a -
C/E D/F# C/E Dsus D
bove or be - side Him. We know, oh, God is in con - trol.
C/E Dsus D C/E
Oh, God is in con - trol. Oh,

God is in __ con - trol. __ Oh, _____ God is in __ con - trol.

THE WARRIOR IS A CHILD

Words and Music by
TWILA PARIS

Moderately

Late - ly___ I've ___ been win - ning bat - tles left ___ and right.
Un - a - fraid ___ be - cause His ar - mor is ___ the best.

But e - ven ___ win - ners can get
But e - ven ___ sol - diers need a

wound - ed in ___ the fight.
qui - et place ___ to rest.

Peo - ple say ___ that I'm ___
Peo - ple say ___ that I'm ___

D/F#
G
D(add9)/F#
— a - ma - zing, — strong be - yond — my years. — But
— a - ma - zing, — nev - er face — re - treat. — But
Em7
D/F#
G
Asus
they don't see — in - side — of me I'm hid - ing all — the tears. —
they don't see — the en - e - mies that lay me at — His feet. —
D
F#m
They don't know — that I go run - ning home —
G
A
D
— when I — fall down. — They don't know who

picks me up___ when ___ one is___ a - round.___ I

drop my sword and cry___ for just ___ a - while,___

'cause deep in - side ___ this ar - mor ___

___ the war - rior is___ a child. ___

They don't
know _____ that I go run-ning home ___ when I ___ fall down.___

They don't know___ who picks me up___ when no___

___ one is___ a-round.___ I drop my sword and

look up for ___ a smile, ___ 'cause

deep in-side ___ this ar - mor, _____ deep___ in-side,

deep in - side ___ this ar - mor, ___ deep in -

side ___ this ar - mor, ___ deep in - side ___ this ar -

- mor, ___ deep in - side ___ this ar -

- mor, ___ the war - rior is ___ a child. ___

La la la la _____ la la la la la _____

la la _____ la. _____ The

war - rior is _____ a child. _____

RUNNER

Words and Music by TWILA PARIS
and STARLA ORENE PARIS

Moderately slow

Cour-i-er val-iant, bear-ing the flame,___
Ob-sta-cle an-cient, chill-ing the way,___

mes-sen-ger no-ble sent in His name;___ Fast-er and hard-er
en-e-my wak-ened stok-ing the fray;___ Still be de-ter-mined

run through the night,___ des-per-ate re-lay
fear-less and true,___ lift high the stand-ard

car - ry the light,_____ car - ry the light._____
car - ry it through,_____ car - ry it through._____

Run - ner,_____ when the road is long_____ feel like

giv - ing in,_____ but you're hang - in' on,_____ Oh, run - ner,_____ when the

2nd time to Coda

race is won_____ you will run in - to_____ His arms._____

Mind - ful of man - y wait - ing to run,____ des - tined to fin-

- ish what you've be - gun;____ Mil - lions be - fore____ you cheer - ing you on,____

God - speed, dear run - ner, car - ry it home, _____

car - ry it home. _____

Run - ner, ____ when the

road is long, ____ feel like giv - ing in, ____ But you're hang - in' on.___ Oh, run - ner,___ when the race is won___ you will

run in - to___ His arms.___

SPARKS AND SHADOWS

Words and Music by
TWILA PARIS

With a steady beat

Cov - er the dis - tance, love in be - tween us
Car - ry the mes - sage deep in the hol - low,
You are the on - ly truth in ex - ist - ence.

when I am cold ___ and a - fraid. ___
hide it a - way ___ un - der - ground. ___
Why would I reach ___ for more? ___

You are the se - cret spok - en in ___ si - lence,
There is a wea - ry con - fi - dence ___ fad - ing.
You are my fu - ture, here in the ___ pres - ent,

keep - ing the vow ___ You have made. ___
When it is lost ___ I am found. ___
all that has gone ___ be - fore. ___

You hold ___

me ___ through sparks ___ and shad - ows, ___ You see ___

me ___ a - way. ___ When night ___

To Coda ⊕

falls____ and my____ thoughts wan - der, You stay.____

1

I love____ the way.____

The way.____

2

I love____ the way You keep__ on tear - ing down__ these

walls, and bring - ing near __ the ver - y far. __ I

love __ the way you keep __ this gen - tle but __ in -

sis - tent re - vo - lu - tion in __ my heart. I love the

way You __ are. __ You hold __

me __ through sparks ____ and shad - ows, sparks _____ and shad - ows, shad -

ows.

D.S. al Coda

CODA

I love the way __ you hold __

me ____ through sparks _____ and shad - ows, __ You see __

me a - way. ____ When night _____ falls __ and my _

F
C/E
B♭
thoughts wan - der, You stay.
I love the way.
Am
G
Fmaj7
Em
Am
G
Fmaj7
Am
G
Fmaj7
Em
I love the way,
way.
Am
G
Fmaj7
Sparks and shad - ows.

THE JOY OF THE LORD

Words and Music by
TWILA PARIS

Moderately

The joy of— the Lord
joy of— the Lord

Eb   Eb   Eb   Bb/D

will be— my strength.   I will— not fal - ter,   I will— not— faint.
will be— my strength.   He will— up - hold me   all of— my— days.

Cm   Cm/Bb   Ab   Eb/G   Ab   Ab/Bb

He is— my Shep - herd,. I am not— a - fraid,   the joy of— the Lord is— my
I am— sur - round - ed— by mer - cy— and grace.   The joy of— the Lord is— my

Eb   Ab   Eb/G

strength.   The joy of— the Lord,   the joy of— the Lord,   the
strength.

joy of— the Lord is— my strength.

The strength. The strength.

joy of— the Lord will be— my strength. I will— not wai - ver,

F   C/E   Dm   Dm/C

walk - ing— by— faith.   He will— be strong to— de -

Bb   F/A   Bb   Bb/C

li - ver— me safe.   The joy of— the Lord is— my

F   Bb   F/A

strength.   The joy of— the Lord,   the joy of— the Lord,   the

Repeat 4 x

joy of— the Lord is— my strength. The

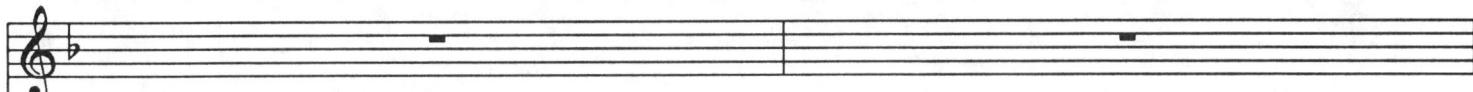

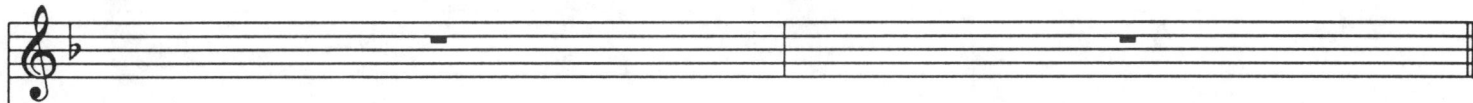

WE WILL GLORIFY

Words and Music by
TWILA PARIS

With dignity

mf

1. We will glo-ri-fy the
(2) ho-vah reigns in

King of Kings, we will glo-ri-fy the___ Lamb; We will
maj-es-ty, we will bow be-fore His___ throne; We will

glo-ri-fy the Lord of Lords, Who___ is the great I___
wor-ship Him in right-eous-ness, we will wor-ship Him a-

1. Am. 2. Lord Je - lone.

3. He is

gradually louder

(3.) Lord of heav - en, Lord of earth, He is Lord of all who
(4.) lu - jah to the King of Kings, hal - le - lu - jah to the
(5.) glo - ri - fy the King of Kings, we will glo - ri - fy the

live; He is Lord a - bove the u - ni - verse, all
Lamb; Hal - le - lu - jah to the Lord of Lords, Who
Lamb; We will glo - ri - fy the Lord of Lords, Who

praise to Him we give. 4. O Hal - le -
is the great I Am. 5. We will Am, Who

is the great I Am.

WE BOW DOWN

Words and Music by
TWILA PARIS

Simply

mf

You are ___

Lord of cre - a - tion and Lord of my ___ life,
King of cre - a - tion and King of my ___ life,

Lord of the land ___ and ___ the ___ sea. You were ___
King of the land ___ and ___ the ___ sea. You were ___

C

Lord of the heav - ens be - fore there was ___ time, and
King of the heav - ens be - fore there was ___ time, and

G/B   **Am**

Dm/F

Lord of all ___ Lords ___ You will be. We bow ___
King of all ___ Kings ___ You will be. We bow ___

F/G   **G7**   **C**

Gsus/F   **C/E**   **G**   **C**

down ___ and we ___ wor - ship You, ___ Lord. We bow ___
down ___ and we ___ crown You the ___ King. We bow ___
down ___ and we ___ wor - ship You, ___ Lord. We bow ___

Gsus/F   **C/E**   **G**   **C**

down ___ and we ___ wor - ship You, ___ Lord. We bow ___
down ___ and we ___ crown You the ___ King. We bow ___
down ___ and we ___ wor - ship You, ___ Lord. We bow ___

Chords: Gsus/F · C/E · G · Am

down _____ and we ___ wor - ship You, _____ Lord.
down _____ and we ___ crown You the _____ King.
down _____ and we ___ wor - ship You, _____ Lord.

To Coda ⊕

1

Chords: Dm/F · G · G⁷ · C · Csus

Lord of all ___ Lords ___ You will be. _____
King of all ___ Kings ___ You will
Lord of all ___ Lords ___ You will

Chords: C · Csus · C · Csus · C

2

Chords: Csus · C

You are ___ be. _____

We bow ___

D.S. al Coda

be. _____ We bow __ down _____ and we crown You the King. __

CODA

We bow down and we crown You the King. We bow down and we crown You the King. King of all Kings You will be.

RUN TO YOU

Words and Music by
TWILA PARIS

Moderately

Cm7   A♭sus2   B♭

Cm7   A♭sus2   B♭

Cm7   A♭   B♭sus

Fast- er now ___ than ev - er, ___ I run ___ to You.
E - ven on ___ the sad ___ days, ___ I run ___ to You.

Cm7   A♭(add2)

Now I know ___ You bet - ter, ___
E - ven on ___ the good ___ days, too,

I run __ to You.   I __ am a lit-tle old-
I run __ to You.   E - ven be-fore all __

- er now, __   You know __ it's true. __   May-
else __ fails, __   You know __ it's true. __   You __

- be a lit-tle wis-er, too, __   I run __ to You. __
__ are the wind in my __ sails, __

__ And I __ can see __   (I __ can see) __   deep-

Eb/G   Ab

-er than I did be - fore. ___ I do ___ be - lieve, ___ (I ___ be - lieve)___

Bb   Eb/G   Ab

___ nev - er have I been so sure ___ { that I need _
{ that I need _

Fm   Db

___ You ev - 'ry min - ute, ev - 'ry day, ___
___ You ev - 'ry foot - step, all ___ the way, ___

Fm

That I need ___ You more ___ than I ___ could ev - er say. ___
That I need ___ You so ___ much more ___ than I can say. ___

B♭sus
B♭
Dm
B♭
Ooh,
C
Dm
I run to You.
Ooh,
B♭
C
What else would I do? I run to You.
Dm
B♭
C
Ooh, I run to You.

Ooh.

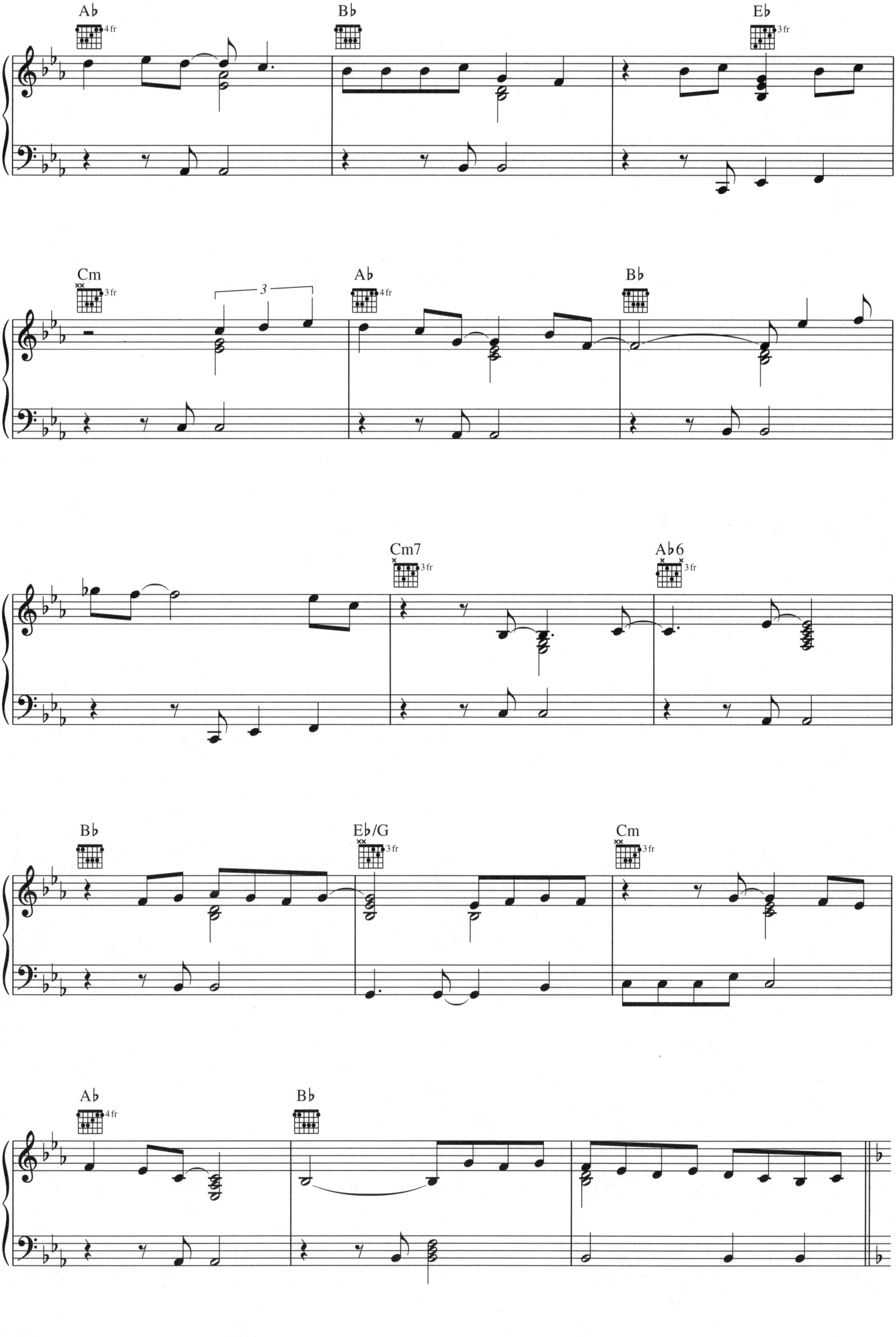
A♭
4 fr
B♭
E♭
3 fr
Cm
3 fr
3
A♭
4 fr
B♭
Cm7
3 fr
A♭6
3 fr
B♭
E♭/G
3 fr
Cm
3 fr
A♭
4 fr
B♭

Ooh, ____ I run ____ to You. ____

Ooh, ____

What else would ___ I do? _____ I run ____ to You. ___

Ooh, _____

I run _____ to You. _____

Ooh, _____

Repeat and Fade

Optional Ending

Dm

_____ yeah, _____ yeah. _____

(I AM) NOT AFRAID ANYMORE

Words and Music by
TWILA PARIS

Rhythmically

I said I ____ be - longed ____ to You, ____ but in a
You have al - ways been ____ the same. ____ I ran a -

Bb   F   Bb   F

se - cret room   I kept a se - cret list.
way from room You, I ran a - way from You.

C/E

I said, "An - y - thing _____ for You, _____   an - y -
Ev - 'ry time _____ You called _____ my name, _____ I tried to

Bb   F   Bb   F

thing but this,   an - y - thing but this." You knew it
hide the truth,   I tried to hide the truth. You knew it

Bb   C   Bb   C   Bb   F

all a - long,   You knew it ver - y well.
all a - long,   You knew it ver - y well.

Bb F Bb C F/A Bb

You knew the stur - dy walls __ I hid ___ be - hind __ were noth -
You knew the more I cov - ered up ___ my heart, __ the more __

Gm7 Csus C

- ing but a pris - on cell. ___
___ I did - n't know my - self. ___

F

I _____ am not a - fraid an - y - more.

C/E Bb/D F/C Bb/D

___ You have o - pened all the win - dows, o -

- pened all the doors. I____ am not a-fraid an - y - more.__

__ I feel the wind of free - dom like I nev - er

did be - fore. The light is fill - ing up the cor-ners, danc - ing on the floor. I__

__ am not a-fraid an - y - more.__

B♭
F
B♭
C
2
F
C
No room for fear,
F
C
B♭
F
no room, no room. No room
C
Dm
C
F/A
B♭
for fear; per - fect love is liv - ing here.

F/A
Bb
F/A
Bb
F/A
F
Dm
Csus
3 fr
C
D.S. al Coda
I
CODA
Bb
F/A
Dm
fill - ing up the cor - ners, danc -
C
Bb
C
- ing on the floor. I am not a - fraid an - y - more.
F
Bb
C
Repeat and Fade
I am not a - fraid an - y - more.

FAITHFUL FATHER

Words and Music by
TWILA PARIS

Gently rhythmic

Once in a while ___ my heart ___
There was a fear ___ in - side ___

___ gets lone - ly. Once in a while, ___ when night ___ is blue. ___
___ my an - ger. I was - n't sure ___ if You ___ were there. ___

Time and a - gain ___ You are ___ the ___ on - ly ___ One ___ I can
Great love would prove ___ You are ___ the ___ an - swer ___ to ___ an - y

hold on to. ___ There nev-er is a ___ mo-ment when You ___
hon-est prayer. ___ The ves-sel that is ___ emp-ty You will ___

leave my ___ side. ___ I felt Your arms a-round me ev-'ry ___
come and ___ fill. ___ You prom-ised to com-plete me and I ___

time I ___ cried. ___ All my ___ life. ___
know You ___ will. ___ I know You ___ will. ___

You have been ___ a faith-ful ___ Fa-ther. I be-lieve ___ Your word ___

Gm7 A♭ D♭(add2) Fm Cm
4fr 4fr 3fr
is true. You have been a faith - ful Fa - ther.
B♭sus B♭
1
A♭maj9 B♭/E♭ Cm7 B♭sus B♭
I will fol - low You.
A♭maj9 B♭/E♭ E♭/G A♭maj7
2
A♭maj9
You wher - ev - er You lead
B♭/C Cm7 A♭maj9
me. You, the pas - sion that freed

Lyrics under the staves:

me. ___ You, when-ev-er you call, ___

___ what-ev-er You say. _____

You have been ___ a faith-ful ___ Fa-ther. I be-lieve ___ Your word ___

___ is true. ___ You have been ___ a faith-ful ___ Fa-ther.

Chord symbols: B♭/C, Cm, A♭, Fm, B♭/D, C5, B♭, C, F/A, B♭maj7, B♭, C, F/A, B♭maj7, E♭(add2), Gm, Dm7

Lyrics:

I will __ fol - low You. __

You. __

You have been __ a faith - ful __ Fa - ther. I will __ fol - low __

You. __

Once in a while___ my heart___ ___ gets lone - ly. Once in a while,___ when night___ ___ is blue.___ Time and a - gain___ You are___ the___ on - ly One.___

HOW BEAUTIFUL

Words and Music by
TWILA PARIS

How beau - ti - ful ___
beau - ti - ful ___
beau - ti - ful ___

the hands ___ that ___
the heart ___ that ___
the ra - diant ___

D/A

G/B

served _____ the wine and the bread ____
bled, _____ that took all my ____
Bride _____ who waits for her ____

D/A

Em7/B

_____ and the sons ____ of the
sin and ____ bore ____ it in -
Groom with His light ____ in her

A/C♯

D

earth. How _____ beau - ti -
stead. How _____ beau - ti -
eyes. How _____ beau - ti -

F♯m/C♯

G/B

ful the feet _____ that ____
ful the ten - der ____
ful when hum - ble hearts ____

D/A

G/B

walked the long, dust - y _____
eyes that choose to for -
give the fruit of pure _____

D/A **G/B** **D/C#** **G/B** **A/C#**

roads and the hill ___ to the cross.
give and nev - er ___ des - pise. } How _____
lives so that oth - ers ___ may live.

G **D/F#** **Gmaj7**

___ beau - ti - ful, _____

A **G/B** **A/C#**

___ how _____ beau - ti - ful, _____

Em7/D
D
A/C#
G/B
how beau - ti -
A/C#
G/B
A/C#
To Coda
ful is the bod - y of
1
Dsus
D
A/C#
Christ.
2
G/B
D
D/F#
How Christ. And as He
cresc.

laid down His life, we of - fer ___ this sac - ri - fice: ___ that we will ___ live just as He ___ died, will - ing to ___

G(add2)
D/F♯
pay the price,
decresc.
G(add2)
will - ing to pay the price.
mp
D.S. al Coda
How
8va
CODA
Bsus
2 fr
Christ.
cresc.
B/D♯
4 fr
Bsus/A
4 fr
B/A
B/G♯
B/F♯
How

beau - ti - ful _____ the feet that _____ bring_

_____ the sound of good _____ news and the

love of _____ the King. How _____ beau - ti -

ful the hands _____ that _____ serve the

Lyrics:
wine and the bread ___ and the sons ___ of the earth. How ___ beau - ti - ful, ___ how ___ beau - ti - ful, ___ how ___

Chords: A/C#   B/D# 4fr   A/C#

beau - ti - ful _____ is the

Chords: B7   Esus   E

bod - y of Christ. _____

rit.

Chords: B/D# 4fr   A/C#   E/G#

Chords: F#m7   B7   E

rit.

THE TIME IS NOW

Words and Music by
TWILA PARIS

Slowly

We close our eyes and won-der how much long - er, the earth can hold the tears of all its
We look a-head and try to face the fu-ture, but find we have no heart for this to -

chil - dren. We won - der what be-came of E - den while we
mor - row. There is a vi - sion that is bright - er. And if

live in the gar - den we have grown. But there will be hope when we
we will be - lieve, it's not too late. For ev-'ry de-ci - sion be -

Lyrics (verse lines):

fi-n'lly un-der-stand___ we were nev-er meant_ to make_ it on_ our own.

comes a des-ti-na-tion. And to-day we face___ a choice_ that can-not wait.

The time is

now to hear the call. From the Fath - er of _ cre - a - tion comes an an-

-swer for _ us all. The time is here, the time for you. _ If you seek, _

_ then you _ will find _ Him, and the mo - ment that _ you do _ seal your heart with a sa - cred

Chord symbols:

G(add9) D(add9)/F# G D(add9)/F# G Asus

D Bm7 G D(add9)/F#

A G(add9) D Bm7

G D(add9)/F# A F#m7 G(add9) D(add9)/F#

vow. _____ The time is now. _____

vow. _____ Now is _ the time and _ to-

day is _ the day. Now is _ the time and _ we can - not _ de - lay.

This is _ the mo - ment _ and this is _ the place for the mer - cy, _ the pow - er, _ the love and ___ the grace. The time is now to hear the

call. ___ From the Fath - er of ___ cre - a - tion comes an an - swer for ___ us all. ___ The time is

here, the time for you. If you seek ___ then you ___ will find ___ Him, and the mo -

- ment that ___ you do ___ seal your heart with a sa - cred vow. _____

Bsus   B   C♯m7   E/B

The time is now. The time is

E/A   C♯m7   E/B

now. The time is now. ___ Ah. ___ The time is

E/A   E

now. ___ Now is __ the time and __ to -

C♯m7   E/B   E/A

day is __ the day. Now is __ the time and __ we can - not __ de - lay.

E/G♯   E/D   C♯m7   E/B

Now is __ the time and __ to - day is __ the day.   Now is __ the time and __ we

A   E   C♯m7

can - not __ de - lay. _____ Now is __ the time and __ to - day is __ the day.

E/B   E/A   E/G♯

Now is __ the time and __ we can - not __ de - lay.   Now is __ the time and __ to -

E/D   E♯m7   E/B   A   Bsus   **Repeat and Fade**

day is __ the day.   Now is __ the time and __ we can - not __ de - lay. _____

LAMB OF GOD

Words and Music by
TWILA PARIS

Not Too Fast

Your on - ly Son no sin to hide, But You have sent Him from Your

side To walk up - on this guilt - y sod and to be - come the Lamb of

God. Your gift of love they cru - ci -

C G6 Am Fmaj7 C/E Gsus G Gsus/F Am F(add9) C/E
fied, They laughed and scorned Him as He died, the hum-ble King they named a
Am Fmaj7 C/G Em/G G7 C Dm7 G/B
fraud And sac - ri - ficed the Lamb of God. Oh, Lamb of
Am Fmaj7 G/F Em7 C Em7/B Am Fmaj7 C/E
God, sweet Lamb of God, I love the ho - ly Lamb of
Gsus G Gsus/F Am F(add9) C/E Am Fmaj7 C/G Em/G G7
God. Oh, wash me in His pre - cious blood, My Je - sus Christ the Lamb of

God.

I was so lost I should have died, But You have

brought me to Your side to be led by Your staff and rod, And to be

called a Lamb of God. Oh,_ Lamb_ of_ God, sweet_ Lamb of God, I love the ho - ly Lamb of God; Oh, wash me in His pre - cious

blood 'til I am just a lamb of God. Oh, ___ wash ___ me ___

in His pre - cious blood, ___ My Je - sus Christ, the Lamb of

God. ___

HE IS EXALTED

Words and Music by
TWILA PARIS

He is ex-alt-ed, the King is ex-alt-ed on high. I will praise Him. He is ex-alt-ed, for-ev-er ex-alt-ed and I will praise His name.

He is the lord._____ For - ev - er His truth shall

reign._____ Hea - ven and earth_____ re -

joice in His ho - ly__ name._____ He is ex - alt - ed, the

King is ex - alt - ed on high.

CODA

G(add9)　　G(add9)/B　　C(add9)　　G　　Am7　　C/G

joice in His ho - ly name. _____ He is ex - alt - ed, the

F　　D7sus　　G　　　　D　　G/B D/C C/E D G/D D7 Em　　D/F♯

King is ex - alt - ed on high.

G　　D　　Em7　　D　　G　　D7

Em　　D7　　G/C　　D/F♯　　E

E/D   **Am7(addD)**   **G**   **D/F#**   **D**

He is the Lord. For -

G(add9)   **G(add9)/B**   **C(add9)**   **G/B**   **Am7(addD)**   **G**

ev - er His truth shall__ reign. Heav - en and

D/F#   **D**   **G(add9)**   **G(add9)/B**   **C(add9)**   **G**

earth__ re - joice in His ho - ly__ name.__

Am7   **C/G**   **F**   **D7sus**   **G**

He is ex - alt - ed, the King is ex - alt - ed on high.

Am7　　　　G/B　　　　C　　　　D7sus　　　　G

He is ex-alt-ed, the King is ex-alt-ed on high.

Am7　　　　G/B　　　　C　　　　Dsus

G

EVERY HEART THAT IS BREAKING

Words and Music by
TWILA PARIS

1. For the young a - ban - doned hus -
(2. For the) pre - cious, fall - en daugh -

band left a - lone___ with - out___ a rea - son, For the
ter, for her dev - as - ta - ted fa - ther, For the

pil - grim in___ the cit - y___ where___ there is___
prod - i - gal___ who's dy - ing___ in a strange___

___ no home.___ For the son with-out___ a fa-
___ new way.___ For the child who's al - ways hun-

ther, for his sol - i - tar - y moth-
gry, for the pa - tr'ot with___ no coun-

er,___ I have___ a mes - sage:
try,___ I have___ a mes - sage:

He sees_____ you, He

knows_____ you, He loves you,

He loves you.
Je - sus Ev - 'ry

heart that__ is break - ing__ to - night__

C2/E
Fmaj9
G
is the heart of a child that He holds
G/A
Am
F
in His sight; Oh how He longs
G
2nd time to Coda
Am
to hold in His arms
2nd time to Coda
G/A
Fmaj9
F/G
Ev - 'ry heart that is break - ing to - night.

C2
C2/E
Fmaj9
Ev - 'ry heart that is break -
F/G
G7
C2
C2/E
ing to - night.
Fmaj9
F/G
2. For the
CODA
Am
G/A
Am

Ev - 'ry heart that is break - ing to - night.

Ev - 'ry heart that is break - ing to - night.

Ev - 'ry heart that is break -

G7 C2 C2/E
ing to - night.
Fmaj9 F/G
For ev - 'ry
C2 C2/E
heart.
Fmaj9 F/G G7 F
rit.

FAITHFUL FRIEND

Words and Music by TWILA PARIS
and STEVEN CURTIS CHAPMAN

Quietly

Female: Ev - 'ry - one knows _____ you as a man _ of hon - or. I am glad _ to know _____ you sim - ply as _____ a friend. _ You've al - ways tak - en time to be ___ my broth - er and I'll be stand - ing by ___ ___ you in the end. _____ But I will nev - er put ___ ___ you on ___ a ped - es - tal. ___ I thank the Lord ___ for ev - 'ry - thing ___ you do. ___

I'll be there _ to pray _ for you _ and for the ones _ you love. _

_ I be - lieve _ that He _ will fin - ish all He start - ed in you. _

_____ I will be _ an o - pen

door that you _ can count _____ on an - y - where _ you

are, an-y-where you've been. I will be ___ an

hon - est heart you can ___ de - pend ___ on.

I will be ___ a faith - ful friend.

Male: I am one ___ of man - y whose

path has been __ made clear - er by the light you've car - ried

faith - ful - ly as a war - rior and a child. ___ God has used __ you

great - ly to en - cour - age and __ in - spire. _____ And

you've re - mained __ a true ___ friend all the while. __

E
D
So I will nev - er put ___ you on ___ a ped -
A/E
Esus
E
A/C♯
E/G♯
- es - tal ___ 'cause we both know all the glo - ry is the
F♯m
C♯m/E
4 fr
D
A/E
E
Lord's. And I'll be there _ to pray _ that He _ will
A/C♯
E/G♯
F♯m
A/E
D
A/C♯
keep you by ___ His grace. _ And I al - ways will _ re - mind _ you to be

seek - ing His face. _____ *Both:* **I will be __ an**

o - pen door that you __ can count ____ on

an - y-where you __ are, __ an - y-where __ you've been. ___ And

I will be __ an hon - est heart you can __ de -

pend ___ on. I will be ___ a faith - ful friend.

Female: **Should it ev - er come _ your time ___ to mourn, _**

I will weep _ with you. ___ And ev - 'ry sin - gle time _

___ you win, ___ I'm cel - e - brat - ing too. ____

I will cel - e - brate with you. I will be __ an o - pen door that you __ can count __ on an - y - where __ you are, an - y - where __ you've been. (I'll be __ there.) I will be __ an hon - est heart you can __ de - pend __ on.

I will be ___ your faith - ful friend. _____

Male: I will ___ be faith - ful. *Female:* I will be ___ a

Both: faith - ful friend.

rit.

DESTINY

Words and Music by
TWILA PARIS

With a steady beat

Bur-ied in the heart of ev-'ry child
E-ven we who call His name so of-

of His cre-a-tion
-ten miss the treas-ure. Still, the voice of wis-

is a deep de-sire
for which we sel-dom find the words.
-dom cries to those who will be stirred,

As each po - et sings__ of search - ing__ for__ his own sal - va - tion,
sond - ing in__ the si - lence of__ dis - hon - est weight and meas - ure.

once a - gain__ the__ com - mon drum__ is heard__
Once a - gain__ the__ com - mon drum__ is heard__

beat - ing out the ques -

- tion on - ly hon - est and__ cou - ra - geous hearts__ will

Lyrics:
an - swer, _____ will an - swer: _____

_____ Do you know __ Him? _____ This is your

des - tin - y. ___ When you o - bey __ Him _____

___ there is an o - pen door. __ Do you __ be - lieve? __ And will __ you love ___ Him? ___ This is your des - tin - y. ___

When you o - bey ___ Him ___ there is an

o - pen door ___ to your ___ un - spo - ken dream. ___

___ dream. If you seek ___ Him,

n7 C/B♭ B♭ B♭maj7
you will find Him. If you
Dm/C C Am7 B♭
seek Him, you will find.
B♭maj7 F/C C Gsus2/B
2fr
If you seek Him, you will
D/C C Am9 G/D
find Him. You will find.

Do you know___ Him?_____ This is your des - tin - y.____ When you o - bey___ Him_____ there is an o - pen door._____ Do you___ be - lieve?__ And will_ you love___ Him?_____ This is your des - tin - y. ___ When you o - bey ___ Him ___

___ there is an o - pen door ___ to your ___ un - spo - ken

dream. ___

Repeat and Fade

Optional Ending

___ Do you ___ Un - spo - ken ___ dream.

molto rit.

GOD OF MIRACLES

Words and Music by
TWILA PARIS

Moderately slow

Ti-ny ___ ba-by, ___ born ___ too ___ soon,
Man and ___ wom-an ___ once ___ in ___ love,

not much fu-ture ___ to hope ___ for. ___ Tears and ___ whis-pers ___
now a sad heart ___ is shak - en. ___ Cry-ing ___ in the ___

fill ___ this room and hearts will burst with love. _ And
dark a - lone cry - ing out for help. _ And

B   **A**   **B**   **A**

gift - ed hands _____ will do their best ___ and care so _____ ver - y much,   but
coun - sel - ors _____ will list - en long ___ and care so _____ ver - y much,   but

F#m7   **Amaj7/B**   **F#m/B**   **A/B**

it is not ___ e - nough. ___   It is not ___ e - nough. _____
it is not ___ e - nough. ___   It is not ___ e - nough. _____

E   **C#m7**

God of ___ mir - a - cles,   come and __ be _____ with us.
God of ___ mir - a - cles,   come and __ be _____ with us.
God of ___ mir - a - cles,   come and __ be _____ with us.

A   **E/B**   **B**

We will __ trust ___ in You   to de - liv - er us.
We will __ trust ___ in You.   Do Your __ work __ in us.
We will __ trust ___ in You   to de - liv - er us.

E

Kind and __ no - ble King, kneel - ing __ in __ the dust.
Kind and __ no - ble King, kneel - ing __ in __ the dust.
Kind and __ no - ble King, kneel - ing __ in __ the dust.

C#m7

A

E/B   **To Coda** ⊕

B

So pre - dict - a - ble, so mys - ter - i - ous. __
So pre - dict - a - ble, so mys - ter - i - ous. __
So mag - ni - fi - cent,

Esus

E

1

B/C#   **C#m**   **F#m9**

God of __ mir - a - cles. __
God of __ mir - a - cles. __

2

B/A   **A**   **B**   **A**

_____   Your voice __ is pow - er - ful, __

nothing is difficult. You can do what we can not.

Your grace is beautiful, stronger when we are small.

You are God. You are God.

D.S. al Coda

CODA

so mysterious.

Kind and __ no - ble King,

kneel - ing ____ in ____ the dust. So mag - ni - fi - cent,

so mys - ter - i - ous. __ God of __ mir - a - cles. __

Contemporary Christian Folios

HEAVEN AND EARTH
Matching folio to the album, featuring: As We Wait • Heaven and Earth • Jesus, Hail the Lamb • River of Life • and more.
00306335
P/V/G
$14.95

TWILA PARIS – TRUE NORTH
Matching folio with 11 songs, including: Could You Believe • Delight My Heart • I Choose Grace • True North • and more.
00306330
P/V/G
$14.95

STEVEN CURTIS CHAPMAN – GREATEST HITS
14 of his best: The Great Adventure • Heaven in the Real World • His Eyes • His Strength Is Perfect • Lord of the Dance • No Better Place • Not Home Yet • The Walk • more.
00306196
P/V/G
$16.95

REBECCA ST. JAMES – PRAY
Includes 11 songs from her album: Be Thou My Vision • Come Quickly Lord • Give Myself Away • Hold Me Jesus • I'll Carry You • Lord You're Beautiful • Love to Love You • Mirror • OK • Omega • Peace • Pray.
00306268
P/V/G
$14.95

JANET PASCHAL – SONGS FOR A LIFETIME
12 favorite songs from this Contemporary Christian artist, including: Been Through Enough • Faithful Father • God Will Make a Way • I Am Not Ashamed • and more.
00306328
P/V/G
$14.95

TWILA PARIS – PERENNIAL
Matching folio to this contemporary Christian artist's album, including the songs: Amazing Grace • Be Thou My Vision • Faithful Men • Father, We are Here • Perennial • and more.
00306232
P/V/G
$14.95

AVALON – IN A DIFFERENT LIGHT
All 11 songs from this talented contemporary Christian vocal quartet's 1999 release: Always Have, Always Will • Can't Live a Day • First Love • Hide My Soul • I'm Speechless • If My People Pray • In a Different Light • In Not Of • Let Your Love • Only for the Weak • Take You at Your Word.
00306295
P/V/G
$14.95

STEVE GREEN – MORNING LIGHT
Songs to Awaken the Dawn
This songbook includes 12 songs from this popular contemporary Christian artist's album, including: All That You Say • Doxology • I Offer Myself • I Will Awaken the Dawn • Listen • Lord of the Dawn • Morning Has Broken • Morning Star • Selah • and more.
00306313
P/V/G
$14.95

DELIRIOUS? – KING OF FOOLS
Includes all of the songs from their latest album: All the Way • August 30th • Deeper • Hands of Kindness • History Maker • King of Fools • King or Cripple • Louder Than the Radio • Promise • Revival Town • Sanctify • What a Friend • White Ribbon Day.
00306254
P/V/G
$16.95

JENNIFER KNAPP – KANSAS
The matching folio to this Dove Award-winning contemporary Christian folk-rocker's Gotee Records release features 11 songs: Faithful to Me • His Grace Is Sufficient • Hold Me Now • In the Name • Undo Me • Visions • Whole Again. Includes great photos and playing notes.
00306324
P/V/G
$12.95

STEVEN CURTIS CHAPMAN – SPEECHLESS
13 songs from the latest by Steven Curtis Chapman, who in his career has won 38 Dove Awards and 3 Grammies. Includes: Be Still and Know • The Change • Dive • Fingerprints of God • Great Expectations • I Do Believe • The Invitation • Whatever • With Hope.
00306316
P/V/G
$14.95

0401